"Till Death Us Do Part"

ESSENTIALS TO HAVING A HAPPY, SUCCESSFUL, AND BLESSED MARRIAGE ACCORDING TO THE HOLY BIBLE

by

Debbie Buchanan Kendrick

All Scripture quotations in this volume are from the
King James Version of the Bible.

All professional photographs printed were Used by Permission Rod Taylor-Photography, Wedowee, Alabama

ISBN: 1-4140-5163-8 (e-book)
ISBN: 1-4140-5161-1 (Paperback)
ISBN: 1-4140-5162-X (Dust Jacket)

Library of Congress Control Number: 2003195186

This book is printed on acid free paper.

Printed in the United States of America
Bloomington, IN

1stBooks - rev. 02/10/04

Pictured above: Dr. T. L. Lowery and Pastor Debbie B. Kendrick

FOREWORD

Pastor Debbie Kendrick has discovered in the Bible and has modeled in her own marriage and family the wonderful plan God had in mind when He ordained that "a man leave his father and his mother, shall cleave unto his wife; and they shall be one flesh." As she explains in Till Death Us Do Part, following God's plan ensures a happy and successful union. I commend her book to your prayerful study.

----- T. L. Lowery, Ph.D
Assistant General Overseer
of the Church of God

This book is dedicated to my husband Harvey G. Kendrick, who is my soul mate that was chosen by God to be my husband Till Death Us Do Part. Thank you for being a man of God to lead your family into the blessings in life. You have been a living example of God's Holy Word in being a Godly Husband and a Godly Father as this book speaks about. I will love you, "Till Death Us Do Part."

ACKNOWLEDGMENTS

I would like to express my love, thanks and deep appreciation to:

My son, Lee, who has brought joy to his father and my life. You have made us proud of you and the wonderful young man you have turn into being. I thank God for the bond you, your father, and I have always shared. May you too continue to seek God and His Ways and when the time comes for marriage may it be for you

"Till Death Us Do Part."

My parents, Troy and Lucille Buchanan, who always believed in me and were loving Christian Parents who now reside in Heaven, after having a lasting marriage and kept their wedding vow to each other,

"Till Death Us Do Part.

TABLE OF CONTENTS

INTRODUCTION

Marriage is to be taken seriously. Anyone desiring to marry or already married needs to seek God through prayer and reading the Bible and reading this book titled, "Till Death Us Do Part."

Everything a man or woman needs to know about marriage is recorded in the Holy Bible. God wanted all people to go into a marriage that would be happy, fun, exciting, and bless. As you read this book you will see why it is important to do things God's Way. God wants a man and a woman to experience Real Love between them that will last in the good times and the bad times. Many people are deceived by the devil about love. You will learn how not to be deceived, but how to find real love and keep it alive. Some couples are looking for love for all the wrong reasons and ways. Those couples cause themselves and others to suffer a lot of pain and heartaches that could have been prevented. In this book you will find what not to do and what you should do for everyone in the family to be happy and blessed. When a man and a woman are joined in marriage the Bible says they are to become one. What does that mean? The answer can be found in this book so you and your spouse can know how to begin an oneness relationship that is so awesome. True Romance is a key to any marriage being a happy exciting one. Learn what the Bible has to say about sex and what a man and a woman should do to keep lovemaking active in their marriage. Learn what a man wants and desires from his wife. Learn what a woman desires from her husband. Everyone reading this book can become educated about being a desirable, loving, and caring companion. This book will teach you how to understand your mate's personal needs as well as their family needs, and their spiritual needs. Learn how to communicate with your mate.

Dreams can become true. You and your mate can reach the goals you set together during your marriage. Learn how God can bring those things to pass as you obey His Word.

Children are a blessing and a wonderful gift from God. You will learn in this book what to do and what not to do during the years of raising children. God tells the parents how to raise their children so the devil can not destroy them. Learn what it takes as a parent to have happy blessed children and how to bond with them for a life time. You will learn how your children will be proud of you and their raising. Your children will also desire to raise their children from the same instructions as you raised them. Family fun is important for everyone to have and can be accomplished if so desired as often as you wish, with little or a lot of funds. Learn from this book how your children can grow up happy and desire to have a marriage and a home life like yours, "Till Death Us Do Part."

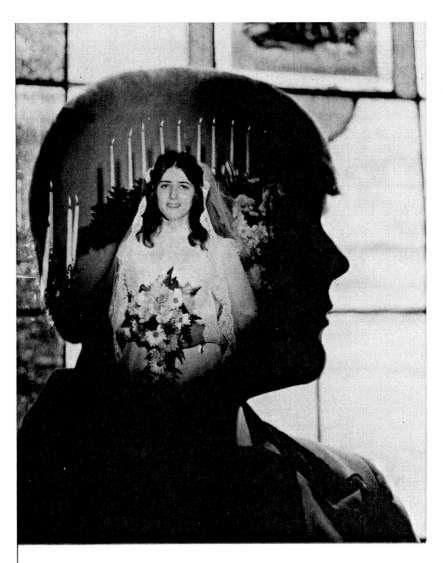

Chapter One:
Real Love

Chapter 1

Real Love

What is love? How can you find the person that is to be your soul mate? These are questions that will be answered in this chapter. Everybody wants to be loved and all marriages should begin with a solid foundation of real love.

I John Chapter 4 Verses 4-12

"⁴Ye are of God, little children, and have overcome them: because greater is he that is in you, than he that is in the world. ⁵They are of the world: therefore speak they of the world, and the world heareth them. ⁶We are of God. He that knoweth God, heareth us; he that is not of God, heareth not us. Hereby know we the spirit of truth, and the spirit of error. ⁷Beloved, let us love one another: for love is of God; and every one that loveth is born of God, and knoweth God. ⁸He that loveth not, knoweth not God; for God is love. ⁹In this was manifested the love of God toward us because that God sent his only begotten Son into the world, that we might live through him. ¹⁰Herein is love, not that we loved God, but that he loved us, and sent his Son to be the propitiation for our sins. ¹¹Beloved, if God so loved us, we ought also to love one another. ¹²No man hath seen God at anytime. If we love one another, God dwelleth in us, and his love is perfected in us."

Every man and woman that wants to experience having real love must come to know God the Father and His Son Jesus Christ. They must accept Jesus as their Lord and Savior. Real love begins with God and Jesus. God is the creator of the feelings and the experiences we have because of love. When a couple has accepted Jesus Christ as their Lord and Savior and seek God's Holy Word for direction in their lives together; they both will continue to be in love, grow in love, and stay in love. Jesus is the Answer! The world's kind of love is fake, and that kind of love will die. The world's kind of love is just a feeling of pleasure that will not last, because it has no solid foundation to hold it together. The world's kind of love is why there are so many divorces and broken hearts and homes. The love that the world gives is being sexually involved before marriage. This is wrong according to the Bible, and it displeases God. God created sex only to be experience and enjoyed in marriage. Not for the pleasure of the world, or the devil's way, by becoming sexually active before marriage.

Paul tells us this in I Corinthians Chapter 6 and Chapter 7.

I Corinthians Chapter 6 Verses 9-10, 18

"⁹Know ye not that the unrighteous shall not inherit the kingdom of God? Be not deceived; neither fornicators, nor idolaters, nor adulterers, nor effeminate, nor abusers of themselves with mankind. ¹⁰Nor thieves, nor covetous, nor drunkards, nor revilers, nor extortioners, shall inherit the kingdom of God.

¹⁸Flee fornication. Every sin that a man doeth, is without the body; but he that committeth fornication, sinneth against his own body."

I Corinthians Chapter 7 Verse 2

"²Nevertheless, to avoid fornication, let every man have his own wife, and let every woman have her own husband."

James Chapter 4 Verse 4 reads:

"⁴Ye adulterers and adulteresses, know ye not that the friendship of the world is enmity with God? Whosoever therefore will be a friend of the world is the enemy

of God."

God lets us know in His Word anyone that is engaged in a sexual relationship other than a husband and a wife is committing a sin. Unless the men and women that are committing this sin ask and receive forgiveness, they can not go to Heaven.

The world's kind of love is not being a Christian and not obeying the Word of God. The world's kind of love is allowing money become a deceiver by thinking it can buy love and happiness. There are men and women who are trying to convince themselves, that they can love someone, just because of their wealth. The Bible lets us know in I Timothy Chapter 6, if you are putting your total beliefs in money for happiness it will fail you.

I Timothy Chapter 6 Verses 9-10
"⁹But they that will be rich, fall into temptation, and a snare, and into many foolish and hurtful lusts, which drown men in destruction and perdition. ¹⁰For the love of money is the root of all evil: which while some coveted after, they have erred from the faith, and pierced themselves through with many sorrows."

The world's kind of love searches with the eyes for a handsome or beautiful human of worldly appearance. The eyes will cause them to be deceived, if love and feelings are determine by their appearance. Instead of love being experienced, it is only lust.

The world's kind of love causes miserable marriages. They never experience the kind of marriage God created from the beginning to be enjoyed and happy.

King Solomon began his position as King by pleasing God. He desired wisdom and God gave him wisdom and riches. Solomon tells in Ecclesiastes Chapter 2 verses 1 thru 17, how he allowed himself to be destroyed by choosing the world for pleasure. He was a man that knew he could have happiness if he chose to always serve and obey God. Instead Solomon looked to the world for pleasures for his body. I Kings Chapter 11 was about his adulterous lifestyle. All of Solomon's worldly pleasures did not bring him happiness, but it brought him heartaches. God became displeased with Solomon when he allowed sin to be his way of life.

We read in the Bible in Judges Chapter 16, because of lust, how Samson allowed Delilah, a woman of the world, to deceive him in thinking she cared for him. He lost his life, because of allowing his physical desire for Delilah to rob him of his own strength and the good life God had prepared for him.

You must seek to know the importance of being a Christian. If you are not already married you need to wait on God to send you a Christian companion. It will be easier on you to wait on God than to enter into a marriage unequally yoked together.

Proverbs Chapter 3 Verses 5-6
"⁵Trust in the Lord with all thine heart, and lean not unto thine own understanding. ⁶In all thy ways acknowledge him, and he shall direct thy paths."

The Bible tells us that we should not put ourselves through the hurt, pain, and stress of marrying an unsaved person. We must trust God, wait on Him, and obey Him.

2 Corinthians Chapter 6 Verse 14

"14Be ye not unequally yoked together with unbelievers: for what fellowship hath righteousness with unrighteousness? And what communion hath light with darkness?"

It is so hard for a Christian to be married to a non-Christian because of the difference of lifestyles. The Christian goes to church, reads their Bible, and prays. A non-Christian feeds their soul with worldly things that God's Word is against. This may consist of cussing, looking at television programs that speak or show sex, abuse, or violence. A non-Christian home life may consist of drinking alcohol, doing illegal drugs, gambling, or having an affair.

If you are already a married man or woman and your spouse is not a Christian and you are a Christian, you already have experienced the hardships of being unequally yoked together. You that are married must continue to be a light and a blessing to your lost spouse in order to win them to Jesus.

Paul spoke about this in I Corinthians saying the Christian spouse is to remain living with the unsaved companion in hope of seeing their loved one saved.

I Corinthians Chapter 7 Verses 12-16

"12But to the rest speak I, not the Lord: If any brother hath a wife that believeth not, and she be pleased to dwell with him, let him not put her away. 13And the woman which hath an husband that believeth not, and if he be pleased to dwell

with her, let her not leave him. [14]For the unbelieving husband is sanctified by the wife, and the unbelieving wife is sanctified by the husband: else were your children unclean; but now are they holy. [15]But if the unbelieving depart, let him depart. A brother or a sister is not under bondage in such cases: but God hath called us to peace. [16]For what knowest thou, O wife, whether thou shalt save thy husband? or how knowest thou, O man, whether thou shalt save thy wife?"

Peter tells the wives how they can be the one to win their unsaved husbands to the Lord, by being wives that care and appreciate their very own husbands. Peter said they needed to be careful in their speech and actions by having a meek and a quiet spirit about them around their husbands like they would God.

I Peter Chapter 3 Verse 1-4

"[1]Likewise, ye wives, be in subjection to your own husbands; that, if any obey not the word, they also may without the word be won by the conversation of the wives; [2]While they behold your chaste conversation coupled with fear. [3]Whose adorning let it not be that outward adorning of plaiting the hair, and of wearing of gold, or of putting on of apparel; [4]But let it be the hidden man of the heart, in that which is not corruptible, even the ornament of a meek and quiet spirit, which is in the sight of God of great price."

Peter also told the Christian husbands how they must love and care for their wives so the husband's prayers could be answered from God.

I Peter Chapter 3 Verse 7

"[7]Likewise, ye husbands, dwell with them according to knowledge, giving honour unto the wife, as unto the weaker vessel, and as being heirs together of the grace

of life; that your prayers be not hindered."

God brought the first man and woman together and He created marriage by joining them together as Husband and Wife. God created Adam and Eve for each other. God has also created you and He also has created a special person that He knows how to bring into your life. That person you may already know and you may not. God wants you to know He is God and believe in Him. God wants you to ask Him for your mate and know that you will receive a mate chosen by Him for you. God wants you to seek, so you may find. God wants you to knock so it may be opened unto you.

You must keep the faith in order to please God. God knows who can bring you happiness all the days of your life. Wait on God. Don't miss that special person that is chosen especially for you. Love the Lord your God with all your heart, your soul, your mind, and your strength. Let Him be number one in your life. Do the things in life each day you know that pleases God. He said, "Seek first the kingdom of God and His righteous and all these other things shall be added unto you". God keeps His promises. Jesus said in St. John Chapter 15, to stay close and connected to Him, like a vine and a branch, and we can get the desire of our heart.

Real love makes you laugh and cry together, work and play together, prepare and build together, pray, praise, and worship together. Real love can be experienced and remain in all marriages. God said, "He has no respect of persons". God is giving you as an individual to know what is required of you in His Holy Word. God is giving you the opportunity to obey His Word. God wants you to experience a love so real through Jesus Christ that will hold a couple together, through the good times, and the bad times in life.

7

When a husband and wife give and receive their wedding vows, and commit themselves to each other till death us do part, they can not keep those vows without real love. Real love will help you hold on to your marriage through the good and bad times, during the times of sickness and health. Real love will prove you can handle life if you become richer or poorer. Real love will cause you to love, honor, respect, and appreciate your spouse. Real love binds you both together. Experiencing this kind of love is so awesome. It only can come into a couple's life through knowing and understanding the love of Jesus. Jesus is the answer for real love. A couple can see their love will continue to grow day after day, month after month, and year after year when they seek the Lord Jesus. Jesus will guide the marriage when a couple seeks Him. The peace and joy that Jesus gives is experience in the couple's lives no matter what kind of problems they deal with. The couple's love is so strong when they both have a personal relationship with Jesus. They know that Jesus is number one in their relationship and they both become wrapped up, tied up, and tangled up in their relationship together in Jesus. A couple can then feel the assurance that they can have the same determination as Paul did in Romans Chapter 8.

Romans Chapter 8 Verses 37-39

"³⁷Nay, in all these things we are more than conquerors, through him that loved us. ³⁸For I am persuaded, that neither death, nor life, nor angels, nor principalities, nor powers, nor things present, nor things to come. ³⁹Nor height, nor depth, nor any other creature, shall be able to separate us from the love of God which is in Christ Jesus our Lord."

The devil enjoys breaking up marriages. He uses many devices to cause hurt, suffering and pain in a couple's life together. In this book, you will be made aware of these devices in different chapters that you read. The closer you and your spouse are to Jesus the more you will believe in your spouse love for you. I truly believe a couple that makes the effort to begin each day with prayer, and pray again during the day, (even if it has to be by phone) and pray again at night, their love will be strengthened to handle life situations. Then the devil's devices can not cause division between them. Whoever wrote "The Family that Prays Together, Stays Together" had to experience the power of prayer.

Real love makes you laugh and cry together. It makes you enjoy working and playing together. It will cause you to be able to bend and give of yourselves to each other. Real love causes you to understand each other and be able to share together. It makes you desire to prepare and build together a wonderful life. Real love is always experience when you both pray, praise, and worship together.

If a husband or a wife is already a Christian, and have read and understood the Word of God about marriage, they must obey God in all things in marriage. If their spouse has not committed themselves to become a child of God by accepting Jesus as their Lord and Savior, then the Christian spouse must obey God in all things in marriage for God to use them. The Christian spouse will be used by God to lead their spouse out of darkness into the light. God is to be first in your life. Your spouse is to be second, and your children will be third. God is not the author of confusion, and He Himself will not cause problems in your marriage. You as a Christian must pray for wisdom in order to be a help and a blessing in leading your lost spouse to Jesus. You never want the devil to mislead you in the word of God to cause you to be a hindrance in seeing your spouse not to be saved. Pray for wisdom and understanding in how to apply and obey God's Word in your own life daily.

Real love for your spouse is also knowing when you need to speak and also when you need to remain silent. There is power in the tongue. You can take your tongue and speak good or evil about your spouse. You can take your tongue and speak good or evil to your spouse. It is in the power of your tongue if your spouse will be built up or torn down.

I Peter Chapter 3 Verses 10-12
"¹⁰For he that will love life, and see good days, let him refrain his tongue from evil, and his lips that they speak no guile: ¹¹Let him eschew evil and do good: let him seek peace, and ensue it. ¹²For the eyes of the Lord are over the righteous, and his ears are open unto their prayers: but the face of the Lord is against them that do evil."

James Chapter 3 Verses 5-6
"⁵Even so the tongue is a little member, and boasteth great things. Behold, how great a matter a little fire kindleth! ⁶And the tongue is a fire, a world of iniquity: so is the tongue among our members, that it defilleth the whole body, and setteth on fire the course of nature; and it is set on fire of hell."

Many couples through anger say words of put down to each other, and it causes wounds in the heart that only Jesus can heal. Satan uses words of anger to destroy couples love for each other, and causes them to sometimes to give up on their marriages. You must realize the devil loves to use the tongue as an evil device to destroy couples love for each other. You must learn to take control of the tongue in heated situations, and bridle it, by making it stop responding openly to bring attack on your spouse and others. Do what Jesus would do. Do good, speak well, and show goodness to the person you love. If you are too mad or upset to do this automatically, then get on your knees before God, and pray for help and strength. There is power in prayer. After praying and talking to God, then go, and show the love of God that has taken control of you to your spouse. Begin to show love and speak kind words of appreciation to your spouse. If you are a wife, tell your husband how blessed you are to have him in your life. You may say things to him like, "Honey, you make my life so wonderful." You may say "I never want to be without you in my life." Praise your husband, "Honey, thank you for being a faithful man and loving me." Continue to praise him by saying, "I want you to know you are a wonderful man that fulfills the needs in my life." Continue to build your husband up by saying, "You make our surroundings a home filled with love by being the provider you are, by earning honest wages in the work force world."

If you are a husband, a woman always desires to be appreciated in their efforts to please their husbands. Husbands, tell your wife how special she is to you. Wives love sweet talk. Wives love to be held in their husband's arms. Wives love to have their husbands talk and share with them their feelings of love and appreciation. Wives love to be touched in a caring way without it always being in a sexual way. This kind of touch during conversation time could be rubbing the wife's arm, shoulder, neck, or back. It makes the wife relax, but also feel a feeling of appreciation and love. Husbands, if you have not practiced expressing your love other than sex, you are causing your wives' physical and mental needs not be meet. Sharing love is desired by all wives through touch, kissing, hugging, communication, appreciation, and understanding. Real love is to cover each other's needs without sexual experiences, and also with sexual experiences. Some husbands take their wife for granted by never taking the time to listen to them, to communicate with them, to tell them daily how they are loved, or how beautiful they look. Some wives are never told enough, how wonderful they are to help inside and outside the home to be a homemaker, and help in providing to pay the monthly bills. Men and women can use the smallest member of their bodies which is the tongue to speak good or evil. Speaking good turns life into a good day. Speaking evil causes life to be a miserable, unhappy, and undesired day.

James speaks about the importance of having control of your tongue and being careful with the words that are released from our mouths, because the words said not only affects the person that is releasing them, but it also effects the receiver of the words.

James Chapter 1 Verses 19-26

"¹⁹Wherefore, my beloved brethren, let every man be swift to hear, slow to speak, slow to wrath: ²⁰For the wrath of man worketh not the righteousness of God. ²¹Wherefore lay apart all filthiness, and superfluity of naughtiness, and receive with meekness the ingrafted word, which is able to save your souls. ²²But be ye doers of the word, and not hearers only, deceiving your own selves. ²³For if any be a hearer of the word, and not a doer, he is like unto a man beholding his natural face in a glass: ²⁴For he beholdeth himself, and goeth his way, and straightway forgetteth what matter of man he was. ²⁵But whoso looketh into the perfect law of liberty, and continueth therein, he being not a forgetful hearer, but a doer of the work, this man shall be blessed in his deed. ²⁶If any man among you seem to be religious, and bridleth not his tongue, but deceiveth his own heart, this man's religion is vain."

Verse 26 tells us if we don't have our tongue under control then our testimony as a Christian will not be used to let Jesus be known to be our true Savior. We must let our spouse and others experience a Christ-like spirit operating inside of us at all times and in all situations that arise.

Real love looks beyond the spouse's faults to see and meet their need. Never be known to your spouse of being a nag. If you have already been known to be a nag, then it is time to stop and turn your nagging into bragging. Do not brag on yourself, that is a turn-off to everyone. Brag on your spouse. A spouse loves to be bragged on. Bragging on your spouse will make them want to spend their spare time around you. Nagging to your spouse will cause your spouse to stay away from home on purpose. No one enjoys being around a nagger, complainer, or gripper. Love is supposed to draw, not push away or be a turn-off. Love is also a good feeling that a couple that is in harmony shares in joy and laughter. Every couple needs to take time to laugh together.

Proverbs Chapter 17 Verse 22
"²²A merry heart doeth good like a medicine: but a broken spirit drieth the bones."

Laughter makes time together enjoyable. Seek ways to make each other laugh daily. Talk about funny experiences that happen in your life. Do something stupid or unexpected at home to make your spouse laugh. Don't be boring, but make life with you funny and exciting. Your spouse should enjoy the time with you that you are a joy to be around.

Real love between a husband and wife has no problem obeying the word of God as it is written in Ephesians Chapter 5.

Ephesians Chapter 5 Verses 22-30

"22Wives, submit yourselves unto your own husbands, as unto the Lord. 23For the husband is the head of the wife, even as Christ is the head of the church: and he is the Saviour of the body. 24Therefore as the church is subject unto Christ, so let the wives be to their own husbands in everything.25Husbands, love your wives, even as Christ also loved the church, and gave himself for it; 26That he might sanctify and cleanse it with the washing of water by the word. 27That he might present it to himself a glorious church, not having spot or wrinkle, or any such thing; but that it should be holy and without blemish. 28So ought men to love their wives, as their own bodies. He that loveth his wife loveth himself. 29For no man ever yet hated his own flesh; but nourisheth and cherisheth it, even as the Lord the church: 30For we are members of his body, of his flesh and of his bones."

Wives must understand the importance of being submitted to their own husbands. Wives that love their husbands will do everything in their power (that is not against the Word of God) to satisfy, and please their husbands. Wives that have Jesus in their heart will prove their love to their husbands through their speech, actions, looks, and ways. If your husband asks you to cook him a nice home-cooked meal for dinner, do it. When he arrives home from work, let him not find a sandwich to be eaten, because you chose to watch TV soaps all day, and didn't have time to prepare a good meal. Arguments sometime could have been prevented if you did what was requested. If the Pastor of your church had called early that morning and let you know he would be visiting at dinner, would you prepare a good meal then? If you, being the wife, cooked a large nice home-cooked meal because the Pastor was coming, then you would be displeasing God according to the Word of God. You would not be doing what your husband requested of you, but you were trying to impress the Pastor more than your very own husband. Wives you belong to your husbands. You as a wife have a responsibility to meet their needs. Listen to what your husband says and do the best you can to obey and fulfill their requests. That is what submission is unto your own husband, pleasing him – your husband.

Husbands, you took on a wife to provide, protect, and care for when you got married. In Ephesians Chapter 5 verse 23, we are told that the husband is the head of the wife. The word head does not mean dictator, commander, or chief. The head does not mean to treat your wife like a slave and beat or mistreat her to get your way. The head means being the person who is in control to see, hear, smell, and know what is going on in the marriage. The head is the one to do something about the things that need to be done to make it work and be a good marriage. A husband is to be a watchman. A husband is to be a good listener. He is to seek for wisdom in his role as a husband. He is to be aware of the rotten devices of the devil. Husbands must have the knowledge that there is a greater leader over him, whom is known to be the head of the husband, which is Jesus Christ. If problems arise up and the husband does not have an answer to the problem, he can go in prayer and take it to his headship Jesus Christ. Jesus is the answer. If decisions are to be made in the marriage if it is about a purchase or budget or something else, the wife and husband discuss and share their thoughts on the matter together. Then after they're shared together, then the wife has to trust her husband to do what is right. The husband should talk to Jesus, and wait till he knows the answer has arrived. God is not the author of confusion. Peace needs to remain in the home between the husband and wife in all decisions that are made. Both partners need to feel everything is well!

Also in Ephesians Chapter 5 verse 25 it tells the husband how much they are to love their wife. The husband is to love the wife, like Jesus loved and gave His life for the church. As a husband you are expected to do whatever it takes in life to be there to care for, to love, and protect your wife according to the Word of God. Jesus proved His love by giving His all. You as a husband is supposed to do whatever it takes (as long as it does not go against what the Bible says), to care for your wife, even if you have to experience hardships and suffering. When any husband loves his wife that much, he will have a marriage that is so wonderful and beautiful like it is told about in the book of Ephesians.

Husbands are told also in this passage of scripture the way they must love and treat their wife. It tells them to love their wife like they want to be loved and it also says to treat the wife like you want to be treated. Husbands and wives are a part of Jesus when they are a Christian, and they need to respect each other as they would respect Jesus. A Christian should never desire to hurt, attack, or take for granted Jesus. A husband or wife should never do those things to each other at anytime.

Every man desires to have a loving, sweet, caring wife that will appreciate them and fulfill the duties of a wife like the Bible says. In I Peter it tells how a wife's appearance on the outside is not as important as what a wife should be like on the inside. A godly woman is a special priceless vessel. God looks at a woman that is meek and has a quiet spirit as something very special in His eyes.

I Peter Chapter 3 Verse 4

"But let it be the hidden man of the heart, in that which is not corruptible, even the ornament of a meek and quiet spirit, which is in the sight of God of great price."

Sarah was a woman in the Bible that was married to Abraham. Sarah loved God and she loved her husband Abraham. She served him as a wife should by showing great respect, love, honor, and appreciation. Sarah and Abraham had many wonderful and blessed years together because of their love for God and for each other.

I Peter Chapter 3 Verses 7-12

"⁷Likewise, ye husbands, dwell with them according to knowledge, giving honour unto the wife, as unto the weaker vessel, and as being heirs together of the grace of life; that your prayers be not hindered. ⁸Finally, be ye all of one mind, having compassion one of another; love as brethren, be pitiful, be courteous: ⁹Not rendering evil for evil, or railing for railing: but contrariwise, blessing; knowing that ye are thereunto called, that ye should inherit a blessing. ¹⁰For he that will love life, and see good days, let him refrain his tongue from evil, and his lips that they speak no guile: ¹¹Let him eschew evil and do good: let him seek peace, and ensue it. ¹²For the eyes of the Lord are over the righteous, and his ears are open unto their prayers: but the face of the Lord is against them that do evil."

Looking at verse 7, husbands are told to do what is right concerning their wife. They are not to mistreat them. They are to honour the wife and have the knowledge of understanding they are different. The wife is not a man, but a woman. She is more delicate, tender, sensitive, and vulnerable. She thinks different, acts different, feels different, looks different, and is different. The wife is the weaker vessel.

The husband must take those things into consideration, and he must do all

17

that is necessary to fulfill his duty in being a godly husband to his wife. Then the husband and the wife together can, and will be blessed of God. When a husband and wife has built their marriage on the Word of God to live their lives God's way, then that is when they both experience their prayers getting answered. God's way is the only right and true way. Jesus is the answer!

Both husband and wife have to come together with love, understanding, being courteous, and always showing compassion in order to have their prayers answered and to have the blessings that come only from God on their marriage.

If a husband and wife are fighting, fussing, and attacking each other's heart, God will not bless their marriage. They must repent with a sincere heart. This is why the scripture said not to be rendering evil for evil, or railing for railing: so the husband and wife must take control to refrain their tongue from evil. It is important for the husband and the wife to communicate with each other to keep their lives and hearts right with God, and do everything in their power to seek peace and ensue it. This is the only way to keep God's eyes and ears on them to be blessed and not be cursed.

Your love can be as strong as you want it to be. The closer you as a husband and as a wife gets to God, and obeys His Word in your marriage, your love will never stop increasing, being fresh, and exciting and real!

CHAPTER 2
Honesty,
Trustworthy, and
Faithfulness

Chapter 2

Honesty, Trustworthy, and Faithfulness

It is important to love and appreciate your spouse enough to always to be honest with them, and then you will be trusted by them. Husbands and wives must understand how many problems and hurt could have been prevented in their marriages, if they had begun and ended everyday being honest with each other. Christians are to be Christ-like. Jesus was always honest and trustworthy. Jesus' Words can be depended on to be truthful. Anything Jesus said will happen and come to pass to show that He is a man that is trustworthy.

A husband should always be a man of his own words, to be found to be known as being honest, and trustworthy. A wife should always be a woman of her own words, to be found to be known as being honest, and trustworthy. If a husband and a wife cannot believe, and have faith in each other, then the devil will use every device he can to destroy their marriage. The devil uses lies as a weapon of deceit. The devil is the father of lies, for there is no truth found in him. When a husband or a wife feels a need to not be honest, but to lie to each other, then one lie will lead to another lie, and then the marriage will be caught up in lies.

I Kings Chapter 2 Verse 4
"That the Lord may continue his word which he spake concerning me, saying, If thy children take heed to their way, to walk before me in truth with all their heart and with all their soul, there shall not fail thee (said he) a man on the throne of Israel."

I Thessalonians Chapter 4 Verse 12

"¹²That ye may walk honestly toward them that are without, and that ye may have lack of nothing."

Being able to believe in the man or woman you are married to is just as important as being in love with them. A person that is not honest, and trustworthy, will not be faithful to their wedding vows.

If you are not already married, and you see the person you care about making decisions that are wrong to try to satisfy themselves, that should be a warning sign for you to be alert that he or she is not an honest person. Are lies being told to get their way. You may notice he or she is always making excuses for not doing the things they had committed themselves to do. If that person does not change their ways before marriage, most likely they won't after marriage, unless they get truly saved, and obey the Word of God.

Every man and woman wants a spouse they can trust in every way. In order for someone to be trusted it has to begin by being honest. A man and a woman should always prove to themselves as well as others that they are honest and can be trusted people. Showing respect to each other by not invading on areas that are personal or private is a way to show you can be trusted. Honest people get respect in their homes, in their church, in the public eye, and on their jobs. When a husband or wife is living their life by being honest in everything they do they gain trust from their spouse. Every spouse should appreciate and believe in their husband or wife until they prove or have evidence that their spouse is not being honest with them.

A good marriage cannot exist without trust. You must be a man or woman true to your word. If your word is no good, you cannot be trusted. God is our Father of Truth. We know as Christians that He cannot lie and He always keeps His Word. The devil is the father of lies. There is no truth in him. Christians are supposed to follow their Father God's example and tell the truth and fulfill the truth.

No marriage will be solid, happy, blessed, or last with a spouse being dishonest, deceitful, or unfaithful. No matter how you have been in the past in your actions and ways, get alone and talk to Jesus. Ask Jesus to create unto you a clean heart and a rightful spirit. King David prayed that prayer too in Psalms after his own sin was revealed by the Prophet Nathan. He repented and started over. Do not continue to be dishonest, deceitful, or unfaithful. Get your life right with Jesus. Get all sin out of your life that causes you not to be the person your spouse needs and desires. Jesus can correct the wrong. He will make you a new creature if you want to be one. In II Corinthians we find that Jesus will change us to be different when we ask Him to come into our hearts.

Psalm Chapter 51 Verse 10
"¹⁰Create in me a clean heart, O God; and renew a right spirit within me."

II Corinthians Chapter 5 Verse 17
"¹⁷Therefore if any man be in Christ, he is a new creature: old things are passed away; behold, all things are become new."

It is a good feeling to know yourself that you are honest, can be trusted. Being honest and trusted, you will be faithful to your promises. This is a treasure that anyone can own, because it depends on how bad you want to be an honest, trustworthy, and faithful person. A person that can be trusted and dependable is very valuable to God, their families, their friends, their employers and co-workers, their church and others.

Most divorces are caused from unfaithfulness. Many problems in marriage cause spouses to seek outside of their marriage for fulfillment of their needs. This is not right and God disapproves of this type of action. Chapter one of this book is about "Real Love" and it tells how we need to hear and understand what love really is to have it, keep it, and not lose it. An unfaithful husband or wife is like a thief or a robber in the marriage. That person is being used by the devil to destroy what God wants to be holy and blessed.

God wants to heal all marriages that sin has entered in through unfaithfulness. God works through His son Jesus and forgives and restores the broken marriage. The couple must desire to turn and surrender to Jesus, by repenting, and asking for forgiveness, and crying out for help. God tells us this in His word in St. Luke Chapter 3.

St. Luke Chapter 3 Verse 5

"Every valley shall be filled, and every mountain and hill shall be brought low; and the crooked shall be made straight, and the rough ways shall be made smooth;"

God loves to do the impossible in our lives. The devil may tell you to give up on your unfaithful spouse that they will never change. But if your unfaithful spouse wants to change, God can turn their life around. God can let you both fall in love again and start over with a new beginning.

During my years in Pastoral work I have seen God restore many marriages that were headed to divorce court. The couples would turn to Jesus for help and forgiveness. Jesus would forgive them of their sin they committed in breaking the vows in their marriage. Jesus would heal their wounds. Couples would start over by courting and dating each other. Jesus would restore their love for each other. Many of the couples would renew their wedding vows before family and friends to start over with a new beginning. God has blessed these couples to have another chance to start over and have a Godly and Holy marriage according to His Word. Unfaithful spouses are looked as being unclean spouses, because of sin. God wants His people to be Pure, Clean, and Holy.

I Thessalonians Chapter 4 Verse 7
"⁷For God hath not called us unto uncleanness, but unto holiness"

God wants marriage to be honorable. The word honorable means worthy of respect. Faithfulness is expected by God, that sex will only be permitted by the husband and wife with each other. The Word of God says the bed is to be undefiled. The word undefiled means pure and not contaminated.

Hebrews Chapter 13 Verse 4
"'Marriage is honorable in all, and the bed undefiled: but whoremongers and adulterers God will judge."

Every husband and wife desires to have a loving, honest, trustworthy, and faithful spouse. You must seek to be those things yourself in order to be worthy to have someone that way. All successful marriages have three separate individuals. Those three are Jesus, the husband, and the wife. If Jesus is not number one in your life, and your marriage, ask Him to take control of your life. Seek Him, and other things will follow that you desire to be, have, and do.

Matthew Chapter 7 Verses 7-8

"⁷Ask, and it shall be given you; seek, and ye shall find; knock, and it shall be opened unto you: ⁸For everyone that asketh receiveth; and he that seeketh findeth; and to him that knocketh it shall be opened."

CHAPTER 3
Obeying the
Will of God

Chapter 3

Obeying the Will of God

Having a close relationship with each other is acknowledging each other's needs, and desires. Husbands and wives must learn not to be self-centered. It is very important to learn and understand what your mate's goals and desires are. This will help you to know how to fulfill their personal need to obey the Will of God. You must love and care for your spouse, by helping them seek and obey the Will of God.

God calls His children into different areas of ministry. Some are called to teach, preach, or sing. Some may use a gift of helps that God has called them to do. Having a gift of helps is a person who is willing to make themselves available unto others. They are always showing all types of love through being a good listener, caretaker, and willing of giving of themselves with their time for others. Some may be a friendly greeter at church or in their community to make new families feel welcome. Some people are called to share in their abilities to be advisors in areas they are familiar in. Some people use their talents for God to be a help and a blessing through a baking ministry or bus ministry. Jesus calls everyone to be a witness for Him. What has God called you to do?

Ephesians Chapter 4 Verses 11-12
"[11]And he gave some, apostles; and some prophets; and some, evangelists; and some, pastors and teachers; [12]For the perfecting of the saints, for the work of the ministry, for the edifying of the body of Christ:"

Everyone is called to be a witness, but some are called to perform special services for God and their Lord Jesus Christ. You must obey God in the calling that He has placed in your heart and on your life to do. God would never expect anyone to do anything they were not able to accomplish for Him. God will equip His children to have the abilities to perform the duties in their calling for Him.

Romans Chapter 11 Verse 29
"²⁹For the gifts and calling of God are without repentance."

God expects His children to seek to obey Him. God wants us to understand, if we do not obey Him, then we must pay the price for disobedience.

Anyone that knows Jesus has been called to do a special work, and if that individual refuses, they become very miserable. When a husband or wife has become miserable from not accepting or obeying the will of God, then it affects the marriage in all areas and there is no real joy. There is no real peace. Problems in other areas of the marriage will surface because a Christian spouse is not in the perfect Will of God.

Every husband or wife that feels a calling of God on their lives needs the support of their spouse. That spouse should care enough and have a desire to help, and be a part of that same calling too. God wants husbands and wives to work for Him together. When a husband or wife shows interest and applies themselves to the same calling, more love is developed between the couple. Seek God's Will together. Support each other in the ministry. Communicate by sharing your visions, desires, and goals together. Reach out to each other with much support and interest in everything that is shared.

I Corinthians Chapter 3 Verses 8-9

"⁸Now he that planteth and he that watereth are one: and every man shall receive his own reward according to his own labor. ⁹For we are laborers together with God; ye are God's husbandry, ye are God's building."

God wants His children to work together in love and unity. God will bless a husband and a wife that will live a righteous life and obey Him by showing love, honor, and appreciation to each other.

I Peter Chapter 3 Verse 7

"⁷Likewise, ye husband, dwell with them according to knowledge, giving honor unto the wife, as unto the weaker vessel, and as being heirs together of the grace of life; that your prayers be not hindered."

Many times sadness will enter a Christian couple's marriage because of having to struggle alone in a God called ministry. It is bad to be without any support from the other spouse. This happens to many preachers. God has given them a job to do and they need the support of all their family members. Some may travel alone because their spouse will not go with them. The spouse may respond "I have no desire to go", or "I don't want to be away from my home, family, and friends." The husband or wife that is called to Pastor a church may have a spouse that hates all the time and demands that this position requires of their spouse's time. This causes many spouses to be bitter and jealous, because of the demands on a Pastor's time. A spouse that is married to a preacher can become rebellious, if he/she does not let God strengthen them, and use them, in the areas of the preacher's daily life in ministry. Ministry that is not shared together will cause a lot of stress and problems. Arguments and a rebellious spirit will show up. God does not like rebellion. Jesus wants us to have a hunger and a thirst to do what is right in His eyes.

St. Matthew Chapter 5 Verse 6

"⁶Blessed are they which do hunger and thirst after righteousness: for they shall be filled."

Jesus gives everyone the promise that by pleasing Him, and by desiring to do what is expected or right that we can be filled. Filled means satisfied, happy, peaceful, blessed, and needs taken care of. Truly when you apply yourselves the way God wants you to and you will see great results from it. When you are fulfilling the need of your spouse in being a part of their ministry they are called into, you will experience a harvest of love and blessings from God. You will reap what you sow, good or bad.

Galatians Chapter 6 Verses 7-10

"⁷Be not deceived; God is not mocked: for whatsoever a man soweth, that shall he also reap. ⁸For he that soweth to his flesh shall of the flesh reap corruption; but he that soweth to the Spirit shall of the Spirit reap life everlasting. ⁹And let us not be weary in well-doing: for in due season we shall reap, if we faint not. ¹⁰As we have therefore opportunity, let us do good unto all men, especially unto them who are of the household of faith."

Every man and woman that is married desires a happy marriage. Reaping in a marriage depends on what you sow. If you sow love, you will reap love. If you sow time given of yourself to make your spouse happy, you will reap time of satisfaction to yourself. If you sow obeying the Will of God, you will reap blessings from God. Blessings from God can be prayers answered when you least expect it. God does not forget what we pray or desire for Him to do. God is faithful to keep all of His promises. God wants obedient children. When we read the Bible and hear God speak through His Word to us. He wants us not only to listen, but obey. God's Word in the Bible tells us how marriage is to be in operation in every husband and wife's life. When you base your marriage on the Word of God you are obeying the Will of God concerning your marriage.

I Corinthians Chapter 7 Verses 23-24

"²³Ye are bought with a price; be not ye the servants of men. ²⁴Brethren, let every man, wherein he is called, therein abide with God."

When a man or woman pleases God according to His Word in marriage, they will experience joy, peace, and the happiness of being in the Will of God in marriage and see the great results of blessings from God during their lifetime together.

Chapter 4:
A Couple-Being One

Chapter 4

A Couple – Being One

A marriage that desires love, joy, and peace will be couples who will seek to experience coming together as one. It was God's plan in the beginning for the husband and wife to come together as one flesh.

Genesis Chapter 2 Verse 24
"²⁴Therefore shall a man leave his father and his mother, and shall cleave unto his wife: and they shall be one flesh."

Ephesians Chapter 5 Verse 31
"³¹For this cause shall a man leave his father and mother and shall be joined unto his wife, and they two shall be one flesh."

God's Word gives a message to the man to begin his life in marriage by being a husband that is taking on manhood to be the caretaker, the decision maker, the provider, and the leader in the ways and desires of God. This is the reason man is to be called the head in the marriage. The head sees, hears, thinks, smells, and speaks. The husband being the man known in God's Word as the head, no longer is to depend on his father or mother to be in control of his life. The parents are not to be permitted to interfere in their son's life as being the head of his own marriage. God's word said the man is to leave his father and mother and cleave unto his wife. God wants the man to stand on his own two feet, in the position of being a husband in his own home, and not be depended on his parents. God wants every son to always love and show honor to his parents, and care for them. God does not want the husband to allow his parents control his own marriage in anyway. Jesus spoke of this again in the New Testament, so the husband and wife could come together in marriage and be one.

Matthew Chapter 19 Verses 4-6

"'And he answered and said unto them, Have ye not read, that he which made them at the beginning made them male and female, ⁵And said, For this cause shall a man leave father and mother, and shall cleave to his wife: and they twain shall be one flesh? ⁶Wherefore they are no more twain, but one flesh. What therefore God hath joined together, let not man put asunder."

Jesus wanted the people to hear and understand God's Word. Verse six said, "wherefore they are no more twain," meaning the couple is no longer to be known as two separate individuals in being selfish or self-centered. Verse six said, "one flesh," one flesh means the husband is to seek the desires, needs, and thoughts of his wife. The wife is to seek the desires, needs, and thoughts of the husband. The husband and the wife are to seek to know the things that the other spouse feels or desires. The couple should communicate and come together in unity and love. Searching ways to see things happen together will bring it to pass through their love for each other. Joy will be experienced because of working together and the Peace of God will be upon both of them.

Jesus spoke about God the Father and Himself the Son as being one in St. John.

St. John Chapter 10 Verse 30

"³⁰I and my Father are one."

Jesus wanted us to understand even though they were two separate individuals they come together to work as one in all things. The Father, the Son, and the Holy Ghost work in unity. Everything that the Father God is involved in and does, He is not alone, because the Son Jesus and the Holy Ghost is a part of what the Father does. Jesus never does anything without God our Father, and the Holy Ghost. When the Holy Ghost's presence is near and doing his work among us, God our Father and Jesus His Son is in agreement to the working of the Holy Ghost. Three separate individuals, God the Father, Jesus the Son, and the Holy Ghost come together in all things as one.

Being one is a beautiful experience. When you as a husband and a wife can pray together, believe together, and see God move in your lives together. Oneness means to agree together. The husband is the head of the wife. The head thinks, sees, hears, smells, and speaks. Husbands are to be a watchman at all times. They are to seek for wisdom in order to know what to do or say. They are to be good listeners and to have ears that can hear God at all times. The husband must be able to smell in the spirit, the good things that is right to please God, and also recognized the rotten things that the devil sends toward his marriage. The husband can take authority over the devil by speaking the name of Jesus! The husband is to speak the Word of God over his family and home. Wives look at what God speaks to you in the book of Ephesians.

Ephesians Chapter 5 Verse 22

"22Wives, submit yourselves unto your own husbands, as unto the Lord."

Submit means to obey. Submit (obey) that husband like you would Jesus. Wife, your husband is to be the head, as God has given him the order to be and you the wife must respect him, love him, and obey him in the Lord. Communication is important in a marriage as food is for the body to survive. If a couple does not talk and share with each other, they cannot have an oneness relationship. A husband and a wife must function and work together in making decisions, goals, and desires. To be one flesh as a husband and a wife is important and needed to have a happy and long life together. Inside your body, under your skin, you have blood vessels, and veins, and you have the blood itself. One cannot operate without the other to keep life inside the body. You as a husband or wife cannot operate and survive a marriage that will always be blessed with life of happiness unto death unless you come together as one.

God never wanted any marriage to be one sided. God wants all marriages to be whole. A husband cannot have everything in the marriage his way, and not consider his wife, and her feelings, wants, and desires. A wife cannot expect to get her way, and try to override what her husband feels, and believes in. It is wrong for husbands and wives to use their bodies to try to persuade the other one to get what they want to do. Never try to get your way, when you know it is not what is best for your marriage. Sex is not to be used to be cheap. Sex is love making created for marriage and marriage only. Sex is not to be a weapon against your spouse. If a wife's attitude to her husband is "I will not sleep with you tonight if you don't do what I want or if you don't purchase me what I ask for." That woman is using her body like a prostitute. That woman is not seeking an oneness in her marriage with her husband. Husbands are not to be selfish, or self-centered either to hurt or harm their wives in anyway to get their way in a marriage. If a husband is thinking only about themselves there is no oneness relationship between him and his wife.

To be able to become as one in your relationship in marriage you must pray and seek God together for true wisdom. When you come across a problem and together you discuss it and seek God for the answer. Learn to trust and wait on God. You both will know the right answer and what to do when the Peace of God overshadows you as a couple and you will be able to work out the problem together. Never make quick decisions about major purchases before you pray. Wait on God, until you know you have the answer, and know that the purchase is the Will of God for you both. When God is in agreement with what you want or do in your marriages then everything will fall into place. Living together in peace is every husband and wife's desire. You can do this when you really allow God to create your relationship with each other in marriage to become as one.

Chapter 5
True Romance

Chapter 5

True Romance

Husbands have their desires concerning romance in marriage. Wives have their ideas, hopes, desires, and dreams to have and to keep romance in marriage. Before marriage, most couples took the time to share, and spend hours courting each other. This was time to get to know each other, to build a relationship of likes, and interests, and to fall in love. Christian couples that applied the Word of God to their daily lives, never allow themselves to become sexually active before marriage. They were waiting to come together after marriage in the bedroom, as God so planned and desired for lovemaking to first be experienced. It is a time of experiencing the joy of the Lord in another holy and pure way. Men and women, that did not wait till they were married to be sexually active, never knew how wonderful that first honeymoon night together could be. Their first sexual encounter of intimacy together could not be experienced in the Joy of the Lord in that special holy and pure way, because of the sin that they had engage in sexually before marriage.

After a couple is married, romance is needed, and expected to keep the marriage alive. A husband wants his wife to meet his sexual desires. A wife is supposed to do that for her husband if she is physically able in her body to do so according to the Word of God. A husband is to also satisfy his wife in all the ways that pleases her if he is physically able in his body to do so according to the Word of God.

I Corinthians Chapter 7 Verses 3-5
"³Let the husband render unto the wife due benevolence: and likewise also

the wife unto the husband. ⁴The wife hath not power of her own body, but the husband: and likewise also the husband hath not power of his own body, but the wife. ⁵Defraud ye not one the other, except it be with consent for a time, that ye may give yourselves to fasting and prayer; and come together again, that Satan tempt ye not for you incontinency."

Verse five tells husbands and wives to not stay apart sexually except during the time they fast and pray. After the time of fasting and prayer days are completed, they are to return to their bed together. Then Satan could not be given an opportunity to bring an attack on the spouses, to cause division or separation in their oneness relationship.

I want all husbands to understand in this chapter that a woman enjoys the sexual experiences as a wife, but they are created to need romancing in other ways. A woman loves to feel loved and needed even without a sexual experience of making love in the bedroom. She desires her husband to do many of things he did for her during their courting days. She wants to feel important to him. She wants to feel special, precious, beautiful, and priceless to him. She desires to be held in his arms, be smiled at, winked at, and kissed. A wife enjoys her husband acknowledging she is in his presence in the public eye by holding her hand and being near her. She loves the feelings she experiences, through the warmth of her husband's hands, touching or rubbing her neck, or shoulders, inside, or outside, their home. The wife loves to receive surprise gifts, or flowers of love and appreciation from her husband. Candles are very romantic to a woman. Those candles may be on a table during a meal, or watching the television together. It is romantic to have the bedroom in candle light during lovemaking time.

A wife loves for her husband to care about himself to be clean and neat in appearance. Most wives desire to experience seeing their husband dressed up in a suit or tuxedo. The wife gets to look at her husband with such joy, because she gets to experience her heart jump a beat, while admiring him. She may get that butterfly stomach feeling of being proud that this handsome man is hers only. A wife loves for her husband to appreciate her and sweet talk her. It is a most desired need of a woman, to hear her husband, in his own words, pour out his heart, in words of love to her. King Solomon must have understood this need in a woman's life, because you can read for yourself in the Bible, the Song of Solomon. King Solomon knew what and how, to express himself in words to his woman, by telling how he loved her body parts.

Husbands have many needs where romance is concerned. Husbands desire their wives to be clean, to look attractive, to be available, and to be willing to perform in the bed. A man and a woman's needs can both be met, and satisfied, if both partners are willing to do what is necessary, to accomplish the desires of the spouse. It is important to take the time to know what each others desires and wants are, before entering into the bedroom unprepared for lovemaking.

Hebrews Chapter 13 Verse 4
"'Marriage is honourable in all, and the bed undefiled: but whoremongers and adulterers God will judge."

God wants us to know He created sex to be enjoyed for marriage only. If anyone is involved sexually before marriage, or even with a partner other than your spouse after marriage, God will judge you for that. Husbands and wives if your bed has been defiled, I advise you to get serious to repent with a sincere heart to God and start your new life over as a Holy Christian spouse.

God wants you to enjoy each other to the fullness and be blessed. Romance is not dirty. It is fun and it is right. You as a spouse can keep the romance in your marriage if you so desire.

Seek ways to make your spouse happy. Husbands take the information you have been given in this chapter, and prepare, and follow through with that information, by giving your wife more attention, through words and touch. Remember a woman loves to continue to feel special after marriage, like she felt before marriage. When a woman begins to have children, she begins to feel not as attractive as before. You as a husband must give her extra attention, to bring her out of those depressed emotional feelings, so she will still feel desired and beautiful to you. Take time for your wife. Don't expect her to cook all meals in your home. Give her a meal out at a restaurant with you occasionally. You as a husband will be glad you did. If you cannot afford to take your wife to a restaurant then you prepare a meal occasionally in the home with candles and sweet music. Be sure during the meal time, to turn the home telephone off, all cellular phones off, and turn the television off. Give your wife your full attention.

Wives it does not take a lot for you to romance your husbands if you do it the right way. A husband wants his wife to be fun and exciting. A husband wants his wife to take time for him to appreciate the man he is. Stay off the phone with family and friends when your husband is home wanting to be near you. Be there in the home with him when he desires you to be there. Don't be a nagging wife. Build your husband up with words of love and appreciation. Smell good, look good, and be good in every way. He is your man. He has sexual needs and it is your place as his wife to meet those needs for him according to the Word of God.

CHAPTER 6
Sharing the
Same Interest

Chapter 6

Sharing the Same Interest

A husband and a wife in marriage should be experiencing the love and unity of being one. A husband being a man has a different desire than his wife (sometimes) in things he enjoys doing that interest him. His wife may not have any interest in his desire for sports, hobbies, men television such as hunting, fishing, home repair or car shows. A woman being a wife interest may be the opposite of her husband's. She may enjoy shopping, crafts, reading, or attending women get-together meetings. There is nothing wrong with a husband or wife having different interest, and having some time spent apart. The problem would be allowing that time to consume your family time. Be sure a schedule weekly is agreed upon to have your own individual private time to fulfill the need to be involved with the interest of your choice. Every person needs some private time alone or with family or friends. You must not take advantage of each other by misusing your own private time. It is better for both the husband and the wife to schedule to do their own interest of private time the same days and hours. When the couple returns, they should be prepared to come together for each other, and have completed that self interest of time and need in their life.

Husbands and wives need some private time, or space apart. It will help both of them in their marriage, if it is agreed upon in their schedules. You are living in a world that causes a lot of pressures and stress on the job force and in the homes. You need time to relax, and enjoy yourself, to be able to function correctly in your marriage. Husbands your private interest may be in sports like football, baseball, soccer, hockey, fishing, hunting, or golfing. Husbands you may have a hobby to build things or fix things like model airplanes, birdhouses, cars, lawnmowers, etc.

Husbands you may be learning to fly a plane or drive a race car, or involved in mud-bogging with big trucks. You as husbands can have time to enjoy those things of interest that you love to do. Remember husbands be considerate of your wife, to set that time aside so she too can enjoy the things that you do not want to be a part of that interest her.

Wives, as a woman you have a need to do those things that your husband has no interest in. You need time to be by yourself or with family or friends. You need time to relax if it is to go get a manicure, pedicure, facial, haircut or style, or shop. You may be very creative and sew, paint, or make crafts. You may enjoy being around other women groups or attending conferences. It is important ladies to be considerate of your husband's schedule. Do not plan to have your private time when it is to be family time. A husband and a wife need to plan together to schedule their time apart. It is also important to plan to return back home close to the same hour if possible, so unity can remain between the couple.

A husband and a wife need to seek to show some interest to share some time together. This is a time to relax together, to do things outside or inside the home, and enjoy having fun together. When you seek interest that you both enjoy, you will find it and enjoy it. This may be walking in the woods, swimming, fishing, picnics, cookouts, attending a spa, or exercise time such as walking or jogging together. Taking trips or attending conferences or special meetings can be fun together. If it is an interest for both of you to go somewhere together, discuss, plan, schedule, and do it. This will also bring more joy and love into your marriage, because you are sharing fun time together outside the home. God wants a husband and a wife to have fun and enjoy their life together. God wants enjoyment to be experience, thru the time and funds from their labor of work that they accomplished together.

Ecclesiastes Chapter 5 Verses 18-19

"¹⁸Behold that which I have seen: it is good and comely for one to eat and to drink, and to enjoy the good of all his labour that he taketh under the sun all the days of his life, which God giveth him: for it is his portion.¹⁹ Every man also to whom God hath given riches and wealth, and hath given him power to eat thereof, and to take his portion, and to rejoice in his labour; this is the gift of God."

God wants you to have fun together and be blessed.

Every husband and wife needs to share in the interest of giving of themselves in time everyday, to talk and to be a good listener. You both should not only be husband and wife, and lovers, but because of your oneness relationship, you need to be best friends. Satan would like for you to not take time to talk, and listen to each other. The devil rather you go outside your marriage and find someone else to talk with, or listen to you. Satan uses people outside of a marriage to destroy what God has joined together. Resist the devil and he will flee from you. Hear God's Word, and you will be provided a way of escape from the devil's devices, that will try to come up against you to take your marriage down.

Matthew Chapter 19 Verse 6
"⁶Wherefore they are no more twain, but one flesh. What therefore God hath joined together, let not man put asunder."

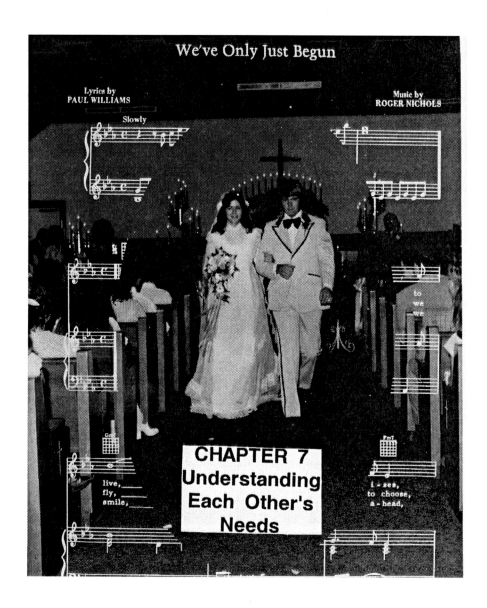

Chapter 7

Understanding Each Other's Needs

As a husband and a wife, a couple has many needs. The couple's desires need to be understood, and permitted to take place in their lives, so the marriage can be happy and peaceful. This chapter is to help a husband to understand his wife better, and the wife to understand her husband better.

A husband needs his wife to appreciate him. God expects a wife to show respect and appreciate the husband. The wife is to not be a nag, griper, or complainer, but to be sweet with a quiet, meek spirit about her.

I Peter Chapter 3 Verses 1-6
"¹Likewise, ye wives, be in subjection to your own husbands; that, if any obey not the word, they also may without the word be won by the conversation of the wives;²while they behold your chaste conversation coupled with fear.³Whose adorning let it not be that outward adorning of plaiting the hair, and of wearing of gold, or of putting on of apparel;⁴But let it be the hidden man of the heart, in that which is not corruptible, even the ornament of a meek and quiet spirit, which is in the sight of God of great price.⁵For after this manner in the old time the holy women also, who trusted in God, adorned themselves, being in subjection unto their own husbands:⁶Even as Sarah obeyed Abraham, calling him lord: whose daughters ye are, as long as ye do well, and are not afraid with any amazement."

A man wants his wife to be proud of him, and he needs to hear love, and appreciation from his wife. Verse six said Sarah did everything expected of her as a holy woman, and as the wife of Abraham. Wife tell your husband how wonderful he is, and build him up with words of appreciation for the man he is. If he is a faithful husband tell him how much that means to you. If he is a good provider let him know how you appreciate him taking care of the needs of the home and putting food on the table. If he cuts the grass and takes the trash out, praise him for doing so. He needs to hear, see, and feel that you notice, care, and appreciate what he does. Husbands have several of the needs in their life that has been discussed in this book already. In Chapter 2 a husband's need is being able to trust his wife. In Chapter 3 a husband's need is being able to obey the Will of God by having the support of his wife. In Chapter 4 a husband's need is being recognized as the head of the wife and the wife and him having a oneness relationship. In Chapter 5 a husband's need is a wife willing to take care of him in the bedroom. In Chapter 6 a husband's need is private time alone to do the things of interest that the wife cares not for. In this Chapter 7 a husband's need is to be appreciated. He needs a wife to prepare meals, wash clothes, and keep the house and children.

Titus Chapter 2 Verse 5
"⁵To be discreet, chaste, keepers at home, good, obedient to their own husbands, that the word of God be not blasphemed."

A husband needs his wife to be there with love and understanding like the wedding vows that were taken for richer or poorer, in sickness and in health. No matter what the situation is in the marriage the husband needs to feel his wife supports him according to God's Holy Word. A husband needs his wife to love his parents and enjoy her time with her father-in-law and mother-in-law.

A wife's needs are many. In Chapters 2 through 6 in this book some of those needs have already been shared. A wife needs a faithful husband, a lover, a caretaker, a protector, a provider, a friend, a leader, a decision maker, and a good listener. A wife wants a husband to support her in the Will of God she feels on her life. A wife wants and needs special attention from her husband to just be near and close to her. A woman needs a touch several times a day, if it is on the hand, face, neck, shoulder, or lips. This kind of need gives her a touch of love that makes her heart, mind, and body feel appreciated. A wife wants and needs her husband to love her like Jesus loved the Church. Jesus did whatever He had to do for the people to have life. He loved the people and cared more about their needs and feelings than He did His own. He paid a price for everyone. A wife needs her husband to do the things that God would want him to do to take care and love her in everyway.

Ephesians Chapter 5 Verse 25

"^{25}Husbands, love your wives, even as Christ also loved the church, and gave himself for it;"

Jesus knew how to love and He proved His love. A husband needs to seek the Lord in everyway to know how to love his wife like Jesus. A wife needs time to spend with family and friends. A husband should never try to keep his wife from her parents. A wife should not let her parents interfere with her marriage. A wife needs to feel her husband loves and appreciate his mother-in-law and father-in-law. A wife needs her husband to understand her mood swings during the month when her body is changing to prepare for her menstruation cycle. Her body goes thru a cycle of premenstrual syndrome (P.M.S.). It sometimes makes the wife cry a lot or feel bad by having headaches or stomachaches. When her menstruation cycle has arrived a wife needs her husband to understand that she needs time to not be expected to perform in lovemaking. Her body needs to be given time to complete the cycle before sexual activity between the husband and wife begins again. Husbands can show love to their wives by being considerate of his wife and her feelings. During the time of her cycle it is desired of most women for the husband to take time to hold them and help with the chores in the home. The Bible speaks about the woman's menstruation cycle in Leviticus.

Leviticus Chapter 15 Verse 19

"¹⁹And if a woman have an issue, and her issue in her flesh be blood, she shall be put apart seven days: and whosoever toucheth her shall be unclean until the even."

A woman needs her husband to understand she does not feel good or desire to do many things during her menstruation cycle. Most women experience a lot of cramps and pain during this time of the month. A woman is very emotional before and during this time mentally and she may cry a lot. She needs her husband just to be patient and understanding and know this time during the month will pass in a few days. Husbands and wives can meet the needs of their spouse by being very sensitive to each others wants, desires, and feelings. Reach out to your spouse and let him or her know you are going to make an effort to understand them and you are going to be a helpmate, a blessing, and a peacemaker to them and to your home life.

Romans Chapter 14 Verses 16-19

"¹⁶Let not then your good be evil spoken of:¹⁷For the kingdom of God is not meat and drink, but righteousness, and peace, and joy in the Holy Ghost.¹⁸For he that in these things serveth Christ, is acceptable to God, and approved of men.¹⁹Let

us therefore follow after the things which make for peace, and things wherewith one may edify another."

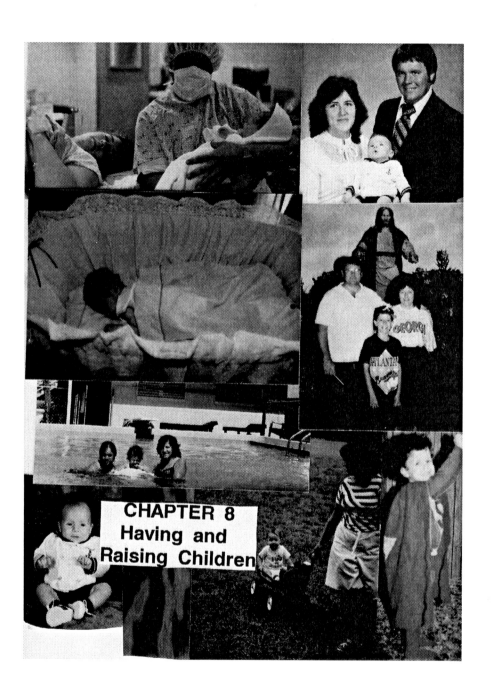

CHAPTER 8
Having and
Raising Children

Chapter 8

Having and Raising Children

Once a child is conceived and the parents are made known that a baby is inside the womb, parents need to sing, talk, and read to their baby. This helps to prepare the baby for their life with you, God, and experience joy and love before birth. Any Christian marriage that desires to have children and the father and mother want to raise their children to love the Lord is to be a blessed family. The Lord Jesus being number one in the parents lives, and home will be a blessed home too. Children are a gift from God. They are to be loved and enjoyed. Children need love and attention every day from their father and mother. A child should feel secure at all times knowing they are loved by their parents. Parents need to be an example at all times before their children. Practice parents what you teach your children. Let them see Jesus in you by what you tell them they can do and what they can not do, is being in forced by you as a parent by being an example before them. Never tell your children to do something you yourself don't do. That is being a hypocrite.

St. Luke Chapter 12 Verses 1-2
"¹Beware ye of the leaven of the Pharisees, which is hypocrisy.²For there is nothing covered, that shall not be revealed; neither hid, that shall not be known."

Children do watch their parents and they develop attitudes, habits, and choice of words while being raised by their parents. They see, hear, and speak those things that they have been shown or heard.

The Bible gives instructions to the parents on how to raise their children.

Then our children can know God and His desires and will for them.

Proverbs Chapter 22 Verse 6

"⁶Train up a child in the way he should go: and when he is old, he will not depart from it."

The best training for your child is you being a living example before them in all things you teach them. Let your child know what real love is by experiencing it through his own father or mother's relationship with each other. The children need to see their parent's faith in God everyday. They need to see and feel their parents love for God in everything they do.

St. Matthew Chapter 22 Verse 6

"⁶Jesus said unto him, Thou shalt love the Lord thy God with all thy heart, and with all thy soul, and with all they mind."

God wants you to really love Him and He wants your children to know Him and love Him too.

Deuteronomy Chapter 11 Verses 18-21

"¹⁸Therefore shall ye lay up these my words in your heart and in your soul, and bind them for a sign upon your hand, that they may be as frontlets between your eyes.¹⁹And ye shall teach your children, speaking of them when thou sittest in thine house, and when thou walkest by the way, when thou liest down, and when thou risest up.²⁰And thou shalt write them upon the door posts of thine house, and upon thy gates:²¹That your days may be multiplied and the days of your children, in the land which the Lord swore unto your fathers to give them, as

they days of heaven upon the earth."

Teach your children from the time they are born about God and Jesus. Pray for them. Sing children songs such as "Jesus Love Me" or "Come Into My Heart Lord Jesus." Read children Bible stories to them daily. Let your children watch cartoons or movies about Bible stories. Let your children hear you pray. Let your children experience you singing, praising God, and worshipping God while you are cooking, cleaning, working on or washing your car, working in the yard or gardening. Let your children experience the joy of the Lord on you while you are driving your car by listening to gospel music or preaching. Include your children in a time of worship by just having a sing-a-long time together. It is always fun with older children to play 'Name that Tune'. A child or an adult is to hum a gospel tune and others are to guess the title. The person that guesses the most correct titles of the songs is the winner. Let your children see your faith is in God by speaking in a positive matter about things. If you as a parent are always negative in your speech, and you always focus on problems and hurt, then your children cannot feel joy and peace. Your children will not have any joy but sadness will be the only thing they will experience. That is why we must do what Paul told us to do in Philippians by focusing on the good reports.

Philippians Chapter 4 Verse 4-8

"⁴Rejoice in the Lord always: and again I say, Rejoice.⁵Let your moderation be known unto all men. The Lord is at hand.⁶Be careful for nothing; but in every thing by prayer and supplication with thanksgiving let your requests be made known unto God.⁷And the peace of God, which passeth all understanding, shall keep your hearts and minds through Christ Jesus.⁸Finally, brethren, whatsoever things are true, whatsoever things are honest, whatsoever things are just,

whatsoever things are pure, whatsoever things are lovely, whatsoever things are of good report; if there be any virtue, and if there be any praise, think on these things."

Many parents never allow themselves to be use of God to bring peace into their homes. They only pray for peace, but they themselves as parents need to come to the understanding you must seek in order to find. Peace can be experience between the husband and wife relationship. Peace can be experienced between the Father, Mother, and children relationships. You as an individual must lead your family into happiness. Be a parent that shows your family it is fun to be a Christian. Verse 4 said to rejoice in the Lord. Rejoice is be happy. You have heard the song, "Don't Worry – Be Happy." When you go around down and out, depressed, worried, you will only cause that sad spirit that is on and in you get in and on your family too. Rejoice, rejoice, and rejoice. You are probably saying, sure, that is easier said than done. But if you will try it, you will like it. Praise the Lord, praise your spouse, and praise your children. Look for the good in them and begin to talk about the happy times, and begin to share with each other how important life is to have God, Jesus, your spouse, and children in your life. Verse 8 of Philippians Chapter 4 lets you know to focus on the good and speak on those things. When you look for the good it can be found. The devil wants to keep the good hidden, but Jesus wants you to know when you seek, you will find. Make yourself feel good by helping your family to experience a peaceful home life.

Parents are to be an example to the children by being true Christian examples by obeying the word of God. Practice what you teach. Your children may grow up and be just like you someday. Your children may desire to know and serve God like you have done before them. Your children may treat their spouse one day as you have treated their Father or Mother. Your children may treat and raise their children as they were raised.

Parents should never tell their children not to drink, not to do drugs, not to smoke, not to cuss, or not to lie if the parents are doing those things themselves. You are being a hypocrite before your children by expecting them to grow up and be good and obedient, and you as the parent living a rotten, sinful life, and you being disobedient to God's Holy Word. Look what Jesus had to say about hypocrites, that would say one thing, and in their heart they didn't mean what they said.

St. Matthew Chapter 15 Verse 7-11

"⁷Ye hypocrites, well did Isaiah prophesy of you saying. ⁸This people draweth nigh unto me with their mouth, and honoureth me with their lips; but their heart is far from me. ⁹But in vain they do worship me, teaching for doctrines the commandments of men. ¹⁰And he called the multitude, and said unto them, Hear, and understand: ¹¹Not that which goeth into the mouth defileth a man; but that which cometh out of the mouth, this defileth a man."

Jesus told his disciples, if the leader is not doing what is right, the followers can not be lead correctly. Jesus made this clear in the following verse.

St. Matthew Chapter 15 Verse 14

"¹⁴Let them alone: they be blind leaders of the blind. And if the blind lead the blind, both shall fall into the ditch"

Parents should be an example before their children in all things. Show them with your own life what you expect of them. They will learn from you what right thing to say, do, and how to live their lives according to the Word of God.

Children need to feel they are loved and feel secure in knowing they are important and loved. Tell your spouse often in front of your children that you love him or her. Your spouse needs to hear that, but also your children need to hear Dad or Mom saying those three words. Also they need to see you be kind to each other, and considerate of each other's feelings. Remember actions speak louder than words. When you say, "I love you," to your spouse, show your love if it is a kiss on the cheek, or a peck on the lips. Give time to acknowledge each other with eye contact with a compassion caring look, or a touch of a hand to the cheek or neck. Children need to be told daily they are loved. Call your child by name and say, "I love you." Tell that child how proud you are of them. Discuss each day what their plans are, or what has taken place in their lives that day. As a parent you need to make every effort to be involved in your children's lives and activities. Your children will grow up into adults sooner than you can imagine. Life is too short to miss your children's special childhood. You are the parent enjoy the wonderful gift God has given you through a life with a child. Build wonderful memories for yourself and your children. Let your children feel so much love from you that they feel they have the best Dad and Mom in the whole world. Let your children grow up saying they experience a safe, peaceful, wonderful childhood, because their parents loved them and made themselves available for them. Be sure parents to give of yourselves time for your children to be around you at meals, during school homework time, relaxation time, and if possible, bedtime. Involve yourself to listen and help and play with your children. It is good for you to enjoy the outdoors with your children. Take that time to play and have fun with them if it is throwing a Frisbee, playing ball, playing tag, or playing hide-and-seek. Make your children feel the joy of you enjoying yourself with them in their play time.

Taking time for your children will cause you as their parent to bond with them even at a very young age.

Parents your children will love, respect, and honor you if you will begin early in their lives, to be there for them in everyway possible, to make them feel loved and appreciated.

When the children grow up to be teenagers they are to be treated like teenagers and not small children. They need time with their parents to share with them the difficult changes in their lives. These changes can be in the feelings and changes experienced in their bodies. They will have different desires in the way they spend their own time at home and away from home. As the parent you must stay close in contact and in touch with your teenager's daily lives. Let your teenager know how important they are to you and how you love them, and want to always believe and trust in them. A teenager has many influences to make wrong choices in life to do wrong. As a parent you need to warn your children about alcohol, street drugs, and sex before marriage. Tell them how they can cause hurt, suffering, and pain for themselves and others by being engaged with the sin of the world.

Romans Chapter 6 Verse 23
"23 For the wages of sin is death: but the gift of God is eternal life, through Jesus Christ our Lord."

If anyone, a teenager or an adult, continue to sin on purpose, then their life will lead to destruction and they will end up living their life in hell. It is important to remind yourself as well as your teenager of that often. The best information you can give a teenager is real life with Jesus Christ living inside of you. Help your teenager to be hooked on Jesus. Be a good listener. Help your teenager in solving their crises and problems. Set rules and expect the rules to be obeyed by your teenagers. If you as the parent don't have rules to protect your teenagers from the world they will become rebellious teenagers. Rebellious teenagers want to do their own thing. If you as their parent don't show concern about your teenager's daily living and activities, you are asking for a lot of suffering and pain to be experienced. As long as your teenagers are being raised by you and are under your roof and you are over them, you are also responsible for them.

Hebrews Chapter 13 Verse 17
"¹⁷Obey them that have the rule over you, and submit yourselves: for they watch for your souls, as they that must give account, that they may do it with joy, and not with grief: for that is unprofitable for you."

Teenagers need a lot of love and patience. Parents need a lot of strength from God to be able to keep the right attitude and have a heart of compassion and understanding for their teenager.

Philippians Chapter 4 Verse 13
"¹³I can do all things through Christ which strengtheneth me."

Parents enjoy your sons and daughters excitement in dating, but inform them the correct way to conduct themselves as a gentleman or a lady. Let them know the dangers of choosing the wrong partners to date. Warn about choosing the wrong locations to go on a date and how it can lead to bad experiences or trouble. Communicate with your teenagers. Be a good listener.

Fathers take time to enjoy sports with your sons. Fathers find a hobby you and your teenage son can do and enjoy together often. Fathers and sons should share the outdoor chores together at home. Fathers take time to be a part of your son's life spiritually, mentally, and physically. Mothers seek your teenage daughter's desires and needs to feel good about herself. Discuss those things. If she needs help in learning to use makeup correctly, either you help her or get someone to help in teaching her. Help her in choosing proper clothing, because shopping is suppose to be a fun time together. Communicate and be a good listener and help her pray for God to guide her life of happiness as a teenager in making the right choices in choosing her dating partners. Mother, it is important to be direct in making your daughter understand what a good girl is, and the importance of being a good girl, and remaining a virgin until she marries.

Proverbs Chapter 12 Verse 4
"A virtuous woman is a crown to her husband: but she that maketh ashamed is as rottenness in his bones."

Proverbs Chapter 22 Verse 1
"¹A good name is rather to be chosen than great riches, and loving favor rather than silver and gold."

Proverbs Chapter 31 Verse 10
"¹⁰Who can find a virtuous woman? for her price is far above rubies."

If she wants the respect of her date then she must conduct herself in such matter by not acting ungodly. She must know, no man has the right to take advantage of her in any form. Mother talk to your daughter about the wrongs and reasons she is not to touch areas of her date or he to touch her. Explain if serious kissing is to continue in long lengths of time, how the body heats up and wants to explore other areas and feelings get out of control. Mothers, you can help your teenage daughters, by being open, and discuss feelings, that often occur during a date. Share with your daughter how not to send wrong messages in body language to her dates. Virgins and good girls should never allow their dates to touch their breasts or other private parts.

Mother, explain to your daughter what the words fornicator, adulterer, and whore mean.

I Corinthians Chapter 6 Verse 9-10
"⁹Know ye not that the unrighteous shall not inherit the kingdom of God? Be not deceived: neither fornicators, nor idolaters, nor adulterers, nor effeminate, nor abusers of themselves with mankind, ¹⁰Nor thieves, nor covetous, nor drunkards, nor revilers, nor extortioners, shall inherit the kingdom of God."

Proverbs Chapter 23 Verse 27-28
"²⁷For a whore is a deep ditch; and a strange woman is a narrow pit. ²⁸She also lieth in wait as for a prey, and increaseth the transgressors among men."

Daughters that become sexually active before marriage are known as bad girls and are labeled to be a fornicator, an adulterer, and a whore. In Moses' day those type of girls were stoned to death.

Deuteronomy Chapter 22 Verse 21
"²¹Then they shall bring out the damsel to the door of her father's house, and

the men of her city shall stone her with stones that she die: because she hath wrought folly in Israel, to play the whore in her father's house: so shalt thou put evil away from among you."

Women are no longer under the law to be stoned to death for being a whore or harlot sexual acts. God wants women to come to know Jesus as their Lord and Saviour, and to stop the wrongful lifestyle of living, and to go and sin no more. Don't miss heaven teenagers, or adults, because of choosing to be a fornicator or an adulterer. In the book of St. John, Jesus told the woman that was an adulterer to go and sin no more.

St. John Chapter 8 Verses 4-5, 11
"⁴They say unto him, Master, this woman was taken in adultery, in the very act. ⁵Now Moses in the law commanded us, that such should be stoned: but what sayest thou? ¹¹go, and sin no more."

Parents, you must help your teenagers to come to realize they must take control of their lives, and actions, and to stop sinning before it is too late. Remind them Jesus sees and know all things. Parents may not always know when wrong behavior is being conducted by their teenagers, but Jesus knows and he has His way to let the parents know.

St. Mark Chapter 4 Verse 22
"²²For there is nothing hid, which shall not be manifested; neither was anything kept secret, but that it should come abroad."

Parents are to have a close relationship with Jesus that when their children are in trouble, they too will know.

Parents check out the friends, and dates, your teenager is with. Don't just assume, but know. Trust is important to teenagers, but let your teenagers know what will happen if they cause your trust in them to be broken. After trust is lost, then it must be earned. It is important to keep your teenagers in a spiritual exciting church where they can be active. Encourage your teenagers to sing, play instruments, do drama, or help with other youth group activities. The parents that keep their teenagers busy, has less problems than those that has teenagers with too much time on their hands. Parents when your teenager gets old enough to hold a summer job, help them look for one that is right for them that will not interfere with church or their home life. It is good to teach your teenagers, how to budget, and handle the responsibility of money, during their teenage years. This is another way to help them begin their lives before adulthood, by preparing themselves to be responsible teenagers, and it will again help them occupy their time.

CHAPTER 9
Keeping Love
Exciting Each
Day and Year

Paradise Cove Luau
Hawai'i 2002

Chapter 9

Keeping Love Exciting Each Day and Year

After the first five or ten years of marriage you should have accomplished many goals in your life as a husband or wife. Look at your marriage today, are you and your spouse satisfied with your relationship? The closer you both get to Jesus and obeying the Will of God together, the more love you both are going to experience for each other. Joy comes from Jesus.

St. John Chapter 15 Verses 7, 11
"⁷If ye abide in me, and my words abide in you, ye shall ask what ye will, and it shall be done unto you. ¹¹These things have I spoken unto you, that my joy might remain in you, and that your joy might be full."

Having Jesus in your hearts and lives brings joy into the home life. Having close relationships with your spouse and children brings peace and happiness. Never take your spouse for granted. The longer you are married the more love and appreciation you should feel for each other. Take time to enjoy life with your spouse and children. Your spouse needs you to seek ways to keep your relationship with him/her fresh and exciting. It may be special attention given daily in words or actions. Your spouse needs to be appreciated and encouraged in their daily jobs and duties. Being considerate of each others feelings in good and bad experiences daily helps to keep arguments down. If you and your spouse have any type of disagreement, seek to make things right between the both of you the same day.

Ephesians Chapter 4 Verses 26-27, 32
"²⁶Be ye angry, and sin not: let not the sun go down upon your wrath: ²⁷Neither

give place to the devil. ³²And be ye kind one to another, tender-hearted, forgiving one another, even as God for Christ's sake hath forgiven you."

Good marriages have to be worked at. Your spouse needs you to make life enjoyable and fun. Share each other's desires and interests. Try to bring those desires and interests of your spouse to pass. Your spouse may have told you they would like to go to Hawaii. This may not be possible at this time because of the expense of it. You can plan and put together a night for your spouse in your own home or outside by creating a Hawaiian atmosphere with a Hawaiian Luau. You can find candles, torches, and ocean sounds on tape and video. Flowers and decorations can set the mood with Hawaiian music on tape or compact disc. Get a grass skirt and lei to wear. Plan a special luau meal with pineapple and coconut drinks, and cooked Bar B Q ribs and pork. Use your imagination in making the event special for your loved one.

Spouses need to take at least one night a week to be their special date night. They need to take turns in every other week to be in charge of the plans and surprises for their spouse on their date night. This may be a night together outside the home or it may be a meal or cookout at home. Always remember to take time for yourself as the husband or wife to have special time alone with your spouse. When a date night is planned, don't allow anyone to intrude on your night together. You as a couple are to remain close and not to be drawn apart. Closeness is developed from communication, sharing, and availability. Satan desires to destroy marriages by having a husband and a wife to go in separate directions at all times and never come together to communicate, share with each other, or be there and available for each other's needs. You as a spouse that cares about your marriage will make yourself aware of your own faults and the devil's devices to destroy your love life.

2 Corinthians Chapter 2 Verse 11

"[11]Lest Satan should get an advantage of us: for we are not ignorant of his devices."

Don't let the devil move in on your marriage. You must take a stand and make every effort to show love and appreciation to your spouse. When children are born, they are precious and family time is great, but a couple must remember each others needs and take time to fulfill those needs. Satan uses other people, to try to move in on couple's territory, to be available for the husband/wife, when their spouse is not interested or available to their spouse's needs. Some couple's desire is to have the opportunity to be alone to talk, to be around to share and hold each other, and spend time together. Be open to share with your spouse your thoughts and desires. If you have not treated your spouse fairly or have been negative to him/her in anyway, admit your wrong to your spouse so that your marriage may be healed. Sorry, is an important word for every husband and wife to be able to say, and mean it, when it is said. Pray together to heal from all hurt. Words can hurt, but God can heal all hurt.

James Chapter 5 Verse 16

"[16]Confess your faults one to another, and pray one for another, that ye may be healed. The effectual fervent prayer of a righteous man availeth much."

Seek ways now to bring more joy and happiness into your marriage. Improve yourself in you looks, actions, and surrounding. Seek ways to surprise your spouse when he or she least expects it. Bring more laughter into your marriage. Let your spouse be proud of you in the way you succeed in life in reaching goals you set in the church life, work force, and in your marriage. Be alive and let your spouse feel alive around you. Your spouse should be so excited to come home to you daily. You should make your marriage so exciting that you are always on your spouse's mind even when he or she is not with you. Your spouse can experience being so in love with you even if you have been married 25, 50, or 60 years or more. You can feel you are the one and the only one. You are number one!

Chapter 10
Appreciating Your Spouse

Chapter 10

Appreciating Your Spouse

Don't allow yourself to take your spouse for granted. You have been blessed to have a mate in your life: a mate that is your lover and your partner and your friend. Your spouse, like you, will have good and bad days. Be considerate in treating your spouse in a loving, caring, understanding matter, in the bad days, as well as the good. Your spouse may not be feeling good physically. Your spouse may have been loaded down with a problem that has caused them to be oppressed. Your spouse may be concerned about a financial matter. Your spouse may have been mistreated by a co-worker or a friend. No matter what reason your spouse is not themselves, treat them like you would want to be treated if you were in their situation.

Matthew Chapter 7 Verse 12
"¹²Therefore all things whatsoever ye would that men should do to you, do ye even so to them:"

Count your blessings daily for the husband or wife you have. Pray for them. Ask God to help you bring out the good out of them daily and praise your spouse for the good within them. If you have a faithful husband or wife, that is a blessing. If your spouse is a provider, that is a blessing. When a husband and wife can live in peace and not live in a fuss or argument, or and abusive situation, you are blessed. Having a husband or wife that is not bound up with a substance abuse habit, you are blessed. Most of all, if your spouse is a true Christian, you are most blessed.

Tell your spouse how important they are. Build up your spouse with your words. Your tongue has the power to build up or tear down. How are you using your tongue?

Proverbs Chapter 18 Verse 21
"²¹Death and life are in the power of the tongue: and they that love it shall eat the fruit thereof."

When you brag on your mate it makes them feel good inside and out. Express your love in actions and words. The words, "I love you," are the most precious words a husband and wife can say to each other. Do not withhold saying, "I love you." Never take for granted it is not necessary to say, "I love you," because your spouse knows you love them. Say I love you everyday you live to your mate. Love is the key to make a marriage last. God is love.

I John Chapter 4 Verse 8
"⁸He that loveth not, knoweth not God; for God is love."

Got God? Got love! No God? No real love! When you really love your spouse, you can face what life has for you in your marriage. I Corinthians Chapter 13 explains to us what love is.

I Corinthians Chapter 13 Verse 7
"⁷Beareth all things, believeth all things, hopeth all things, endureth all things."

With Jesus, you and your spouse can handle each day together. Take each day to love and appreciate your spouse, by showing love and appreciation as if it were your last day on earth together.

CHAPTER 11
Never Allowing
Your Marriage to
Become Stale

Chapter 11

Never Allow Your Marriage to Become Stale

You must not allow your marriage to become a routine or a regular daily program in life. Changes weekly and monthly and yearly are important. Changes are sometimes hard to make, but is necessary in keeping a husband and a wife interested in not losing their close relationship that they have always had and shared. Children have needs for their age groups as well as do teenagers. The family must make changes over the years together, to keep a close family relationship. Together is important. Plan together, and bring the changes in your home life to pass together. Keep unity among all family members.

Philippians Chapter 3 Verse 16
"16Nevertheless, whereto we have already attained, let us walk by the same rule, let us mind the same thing."

Plan outings for your family that are of interest and fun for everyone. Go together, enjoy together, have fun together.

Your spouse chose you as their mate. You were the person that he or she said, "Till Death Us Do Part." You may have that individual in your life now, but you don't need to take for granted they are always going to be around. Make your spouse feel happier and more relaxed by attending to removing stress and pressures from their bodies. If they come home tired, encourage them to rest. Prepare special meals and serve your spouse during those tiresome times. Male or female help your spouse to keep the home clean and enjoyable at all times. Give of yourself to help relieve tired, achy feet, neck, shoulders, or back pain by rubbing their pain away. This is a service both parties in the marriage can give to each other. Don't just be on the receiving side, but also be a giver of your time and service to your spouse.

Always allow yourself to be interested in what your spouse's daily schedule requires of them to experience good or bad. Take the time to take notes weekly of your spouse's television input, hobbies, church, and workforce interests. See if you are involving yourself to be near your mate and a part of those things that interests them. Many times a husband or wife walk away from the television room, and let their spouse be by themselves, when they would prefer their company in watching a program or movie. Admire the hobbies your spouse is involved in. Never walk around to not know what has been accomplished with a hobby. It is a bad thing when someone else has notice your spouse accomplishments and tell you about it. Sometimes a husband or wife is not a part of the same Church Ministry or Calling their mate is involved in. Sometimes marriage couples don't share enough in communication with each other to know what is happening at the public job good or bad. This type of lack of interest can cause big problems in a couple's relationship.

Remind yourself you were joined together to be one in marriage. It is alright to have a few minutes or a little time alone, but not a lot of hours, day after day, week after week, and month after month. You will grow boring and apart if you do not work at being one together. Share each other's interests with joy.

I Peter Chapter 3 Verse 8

"8Finally, be ye all of one mind, having compassion one of another; love as brethren, be pitiful, be courteouse:"

**CHAPTER 12
Family Fun**

Chapter 12

Family Fun

Families are supposed to have fun. Parents need to take time to be involved in their children's school sports and activities. It is a joy for a child to have a dad and a mom around them. Many children grow up with only one parent. Every child needs someone supporting them, and cheering them on when they begin in pre-school, and also continue being a part of their lives in high school, and college events, and Church activities. Younger children and parents can have a fun day at the zoo. Make it special to let the children laugh at you as being a parent acting like the animals. Plan to end the day with a picnic and a time of throwing a ball or a Frisbee at the park. Small children enjoy parks that have swings, slides, merry-go-rounds, and sand boxes. Make a day at the park special for your children by being involved in their playtime. Swing with them, slide with them, ride the merry-go-round with them, and play in the sand box with them. Don't be a parent just watching or looking, but get involved by being a parent doing what a child enjoys. Play with hot wheel cars or small dolls in the sand or slide them down the slide. Take a ball with you. Play ball with your children. You as a parent are building and making memories for your children to always remember. Pack a picnic snack or lunch or have a cookout there. Make your children laugh and enjoy themselves by being a parent that is so much fun. When you children play t-ball or cheerlead, support them in your attendance and cheering. This helps them feel secure, happy, and proud. Color pictures with your children. Play games as a family if it is tag, hide-n-seek, or softball. Ride bikes together. Watch movies together. Have devotion time in the home and play Bible trivia games. Sing together. Have family Christian projects to do together once a month such as singing at the nursing home or making fruit sacks to give to children and elderly in the community. Collect toys for needy children for Christmas. Let your children help wrap and deliver those gifts. Fathers and mothers need to stay involved in their older children's lives if it is to go skating, playing ball, going to the mall, or a day at the beach. Time is important to be given for family fun. Fellowship and play time brings families closer together. You as a parent can bond with them at a young age and they will always desire to be near you in their older years.

Every year plan a family vacation away from home so you can save the funds for the trip and go and enjoy your time away from home together. Your trip may be swimming, fishing, boating, or amusement parks. Fun can be found if you seek for it, and want it bad enough.

Matthew Chapter 7 Verses 7-8
"[7]Ask, and it shall be given you; seek, and ye shall find; knock, and it shall be opened unto you: [8]For everyone that asketh receiveth; and he that seeketh findeth; and to him that knocketh it shall be opened."

CHAPTER 13
Reaching to
Meet Life's
Goals and Dreams
Together

Chapter 13

Reaching to Meet Life's Goals and Dreams Together

Marriage comes in the beginning with many goals and dreams. It may be the desire to own a home, or purchase new furniture. It may be to get better jobs. It may be to travel as a husband and wife in a called ministry together. It may be to travel for pleasure. It may be to have a new family car, boat, or swimming pool. Whatever your dream is God has a way to bring those dreams to pass, if you are faithful to God's Word and also an obedient child.

Mark Chapter 11 Verse 24

"24Therefore I say unto you, what things soever ye desire, when ye pray, believe that ye receive them, and ye shall have them."

St. John Chapter 15 Verse 16

"16Ye have not chosen me, but I have chosen you, and ordained you, that ye should go and bring forth fruit, and that your fruit should remain that whatsoever ye shall ask of the Father in my name, he may give it you."

Purchase a journal that you can sit down with your spouse and write your name on one page and list your dreams and desires on separate lines. Turn the page and let your spouse write their name and their dreams and desires on separate lines. Turn to the next page and together list both of your names, and share with each other what goals, desires, and dreams you have for your marriage. List each one on a separate line. The reason you list these on separate lines is because you will need room to put the date beside those desires and dreams as they arrive in your life. Husband and wife, join hands, and pray for God to use your life together, and to bless your marriage, and to let the desires of your hearts come to pass in His timing in your marriage. Pray God, not our will, but your will be done, use us Lord our God! Amen!

Matthew Chapter 6 Verse 33

"³³But seek ye first the kingdom of God, and his righteousness; and all these things shall be added unto you."

God's timing is not your timing. God is an on time God. God wants us to do what we are supposed to do as being a Christian husband or wife, father or mother, or a child. God will do what we cannot do. He wants us to trust and obey Him.

Colossians Chapter 3 Verses 23-24

"²³And whatsoever ye do, do it heartily, as to the Lord, and not unto men; ²⁴Knowing that of the Lord ye shall receive the reward of the inheritance; for ye serve the Lord Christ."

The greatest goal a husband and wife can set and achieve is staying close to Jesus, obeying the Word of God, and staying in love with each other. Then you will remain married as you both vow to do 'till death us do part.' If you as a husband or wife have read all the information and scriptures given in this book, and you are taking the Word of God to build your lives together in love and as one, you will have a blessed marriage. A blessed marriage is a Christian family whom love their God with all their heart, their soul, and their mind, who put God first in the marriage above all things and people. A family that study God's Word and Prays Together Stays Together. Always remember a family that truly prays together does stay together. There is power in prayer. Having Jesus Christ in both of your lives will cause you to love each other more and more, year after year. Jesus draws couples together, Satan separates them. Jesus is the answer for happy marriages. To love and to cherish, and honor, for better or for worse, for richer or for poorer, in sickness and in health, were the marriage vows you both made to each other. You promise to keep those vows and to be faithful and love your husband/wife only, unto death us do part. You will be able to keep your wedding vows you made to your spouse unto death, if you take God's Word for the foundation and structure for your marriage. God wants your marriage to be blessed with His Love, Joy, Peace, and your needs and desires fulfilled. You can reach your goal and dream together to have a marriage made in Heaven by the Word of God, by obeying and believing together "Till Death Us Do Part!"

About the Author

Debbie Buchanan Kendrick accepted Jesus Christ as her Lord and Savior in the year 1963 at the Bowdon Church of God located in Bowdon, Georgia. She was six years old. God used Debbie as a child to minister to her unsaved parents. Her parents did not go to church with her. Debbie's Sunday school teacher taught her about Jesus through Bible stories and by using and giving her Sunday school leaflets that had pictures of Jesus and miracles He performed. The teacher taught her and the class a song called "Come into My Heart Lord Jesus". Debbie carried the Sunday school leaflets home each week and told her parents the Bible story she heard and learned about Jesus. She also every week would sing the song to them "Come into My Heart Lord Jesus". Her parents listened every week and viewed the Sunday school leaflet pictures of Jesus and listened to her sing about Him for several months. They both came to know and accept Jesus, because their daughter witnessed to them. Debbie began to teach children Sunday school classes at the age of twelve and adult Sunday school classes at the age of fifteen. God called her to preach the gospel and evangelize when she was nineteen years old.

Debbie fell in love and married Harvey Glenn Kendrick when she was twenty years old and he was twenty-three years old. They both were virgins when they married, just like God's Holy Word says and this book encouraged to couples to be before marriage. Harvey was a Christian and loved the Lord with all his heart, soul, and mind and God chose Harvey for Debbie's soul mate and Debbie for Harvey's soul mate. Debbie gave birth to a son Harvey Ashley Kendrick known as "Lee" on July 9, 1982. Debbie was twenty-five years old at the time of his birth. He was Harvey and Debbie's first and only child. Lee has always been a gift and a blessing to his parents. He began to sing solos in church at the age of five. Lee is still singing today for Jesus. Lee was raised by his parents with a lot of love and attention. Lee was raised by the Word of God from the day he was born just like Chapter 8 encourages parents to do. Harvey and Debbie proved God's Word does work in raising children for them to be trained in the ways of God and they will not be able to escape from it.

God called Debbie into Pastoral work when she was thirty-five years old. The family was a team in doing the Will of God. Chapter 3 of this book tells how everyone is to do the Will of God together. Harvey played the bass guitar and assisted his wife in all areas of her calling to pastor. Lee would sing in the church services and be involved in the church functions. They always shared, worked, and prayed together.

Pastor Debbie was still serving as Pastor to her first church at the time this book was written and published in 2004. The church is Heaven Bound Church of God in Centralhatchee, Georgia (outside of Franklin, Georgia). Pastor Debbie's motto for Heaven Bound Church is "A Church where Everybody is Somebody Special". She has ministered to and saw 75% of her congregation be saved and delivered from drugs, alcohol, and sex addictions. She has also seen members of the congregation be healed of broken hearts and spirits caused from different types of abuse such as incest and rape.

Pastor Debbie and her husband Harvey have traveled during the time of serving as a Pastor to do missionary work together in Brazil, Jamaica, and Peru. They have returned several times to Iquitos, Peru where Pastor Debbie ministered in the Word of God in crusades and church services with her interpreter Elias Del Agualia by her side. Her husband Harvey ministered in Peru to all the children he could by giving them food, toys, and most of all the love of Christ.

Harvey and Debbie celebrated 25 years of marriage July 16, 2002. They shared their love with family and friends at their home church with a wedding ceremony to renew their wedding vows. A lifetime of 25 years of memories had been made; they were shared that day through songs and words of love before every person present. Their closest female minister friend Mary Nell Burden conducted their special ceremony. Everyone viewed and felt the oneness relationship that Harvey and Debbie shared. Togetherness was shown in their love for God, and the ministry, as they stood making their vows and commitment in life. They vowed to continue in love and they promised to live with each other *till death us do part.*

Pastor Debbie was employed with the United States Postal Service as a part-time flexible distribution/window clerk for fourteen years while she was also preaching the gospel. God spoke to Debbie in March 2003 and told her to resign from her Postal Service job that she enjoyed and write this book on marriage. God told her to reach out and help people to know and understand what His Word says about marriage. God desires for families to be together in peace and in love. God told Debbie "I will take you and your husband across the United States and into other countries to see marriages healed". God said the people are to be told to keep their vows, for it is better not to make a vow than not keep them. God wants the people to know and understand He created man, and woman. God created marriage. God's Word tells everyone what must be done to have a happy, blessed marriage with people knowing and believing it will be *till death us do part.*

25th Wedding Anniversary. (from left to right, Debbie, Harvey, and Lee)